Frogs & Toads of No

Billy Grinslott & Kinsey Marie Books

ISBN - 9781965098608

Index

Index

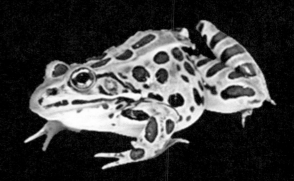

Spadefoot toads live in many parts of the USA. Including the East Coast, the Southwest, and the West. Spadefoot toads prefer sandy or loose soils that are easy to dig into, or small bodies of water. They spend most of their time underground but come out at night to feed. The name spadefoot comes from the spade-shaped tubercle on their hind feet that helps them dig. Spadefoot tadpoles can hatch in as little as 24 hours and can grow into land-dwelling amphibians in as little as 14 days. Spadefoots can produce skin secretions that are poisonous or unpalatable to a predator. When injured or handled roughly, spadefoots give off a smell like roasted peanuts or garlic.

Yosemite toads live in the Sierra Nevada mountains of California. They can be found at elevations up to 12,000 ft. Yosemite toads live in rivers, streams, temporary pools and can be found in meadows, where adult males make small holes to call from. They spend most of their time in underground burrows to keep cool and hide from predators. Yosemite toads walk instead of hopping and can walk up to a mile between burrows. As tadpoles, Yosemite toads eat algae and other plant materials. As adults, they eat invertebrates like ants, flies, beetles, and spiders.

Narrow-mouthed toads live in the southeastern and lower midwestern regions of the USA. The two species of narrow-mouthed toads are the Eastern and the Western Narrow-mouthed Toads. Narrow-mouthed toads are mostly ant eaters. They have a skin fold behind their eyes that protects them from ant bites while feeding. They are solitary and spend most of their time in burrows or under rocks or logs. Males produce a loud, high-pitched bleating call. They can secrete a noxious substance on their skin that can irritate predators. They are one of the smallest toads in North America, usually only reaching around an inch in length.

Western toads live in the western USA, parts of Canada, and Alaska. They are found in mountain ranges and higher elevations, from the Rocky Mountains to the Pacific Coast. Western toads can grow to be five inches long. Like all toads, they have warts on their skin. Western toads have a chirping, duck-like call. Western toads secrete a foul-tasting liquid from the glands on their back and behind their eyes to defend themselves from predators. Tadpoles eat aquatic plants, while adults eat algae, insects, worms, and other small insects. Western toads may spend up to seven months of the year in hibernation during cold months.

American toads live in the eastern USA and Canada. American toads live in a variety of habitats. They are commonly found in backyards. American toads are nocturnal, and they can eat up to 1,000 insects per day. American toads have sticky tongues that they use to catch prey. American toads have glands on the back of their heads that produce a poisonous secretion called bufotoxin. This secretion can be fatal to small animals and cause allergic reactions in humans.

Cane toads are found in Florida, Hawaii, and Texas in the United States. They are also found in the Caribbean Islands, Guam, Puerto Rico, and other US territories. Cane toads can live in a variety of habitats. Cane toads eat almost anything, including animals. Cane toads secrete poison from the glands behind their shoulders. This poison can kill animals that bite or eat them, including pets. Dogs are especially prone to be poisoned by licking or biting toads. Cane toads toxic poison can irritate human skin and burn the eyes.

Green or Sonoran green toads can grow to 4 inches long. Green toads live in a variety of habitats, including deserts, forests, grasslands, and urban areas. Green toads eat insects, spiders, earthworms, and other invertebrates. Both male and females have black spots. Male green toads have black throats, while females' throats are white or yellow. When threatened, green toads release chemicals from their skin that make them taste bad to predators. Green toads have toxins in their skin that can be harmful to predators.

Great Plains toads have irregular dark spots with light borders on their skin. They also have L-shaped cranial ridges behind their eyes that form a V-shape between their eyes. Great Plains toads can grow to be 4.5 inches long. Females are typically larger than males. They prefer to live in damp areas at lower elevations. They spend most of their time underground, burrowing below the frost line to survive the winter. Tadpoles turn into toads in about six to seven weeks.

be about 1.5 inches long. Oak toads can be tan, reddish brown, dark brown, or gray. Male oak toads have a balloon-like vocal sac that they can fill with air to make a high-pitched chirp. Oak toads have warty skin with small bumps called tubercles. Oak toads live in the southeastern United States in areas with pine trees. They are most often seen after it rains when they leave their burrows to feed. Oak toads have elongated, teardrop-shaped glands. These glands house a poisonous fluid used deter predators.

True toads can grow to 8 inches long. True toads have warty skin, short legs, and plump bodies. They prefer to crawl rather than hop. True toads are mainly nocturnal. They have sticky tongues that they use to grab food. True toads are found on every continent except Australia and Antarctica. They lay their eggs in long strings that look like beads on a necklace. True toads have a pair of parotoid glands behind their ears which secretes a toxic substance, known as bufotoxin. This is used to deter predators and can be poisonous if ingested by small mammals.

The Colorado River toads can grow up to 7.5 inches long. It's one of the largest native toads in the United States. The Colorado River toad has smooth, leathery skin that's olive green or mottled brown. The Colorado River toad eats invertebrates, lizards, mice, smaller toads, spiders, centipedes, and snails. They rest during the day in burrows and come out at night. The poison on their skin can be hazardous if ingested by dogs or other small animals. For humans, the poison is a known hallucinogen, that can produce significant alterations in perception, cognition, and mood.

Red-spotted toads can grow up to 3 inches long. Females are usually larger than males. Red-spotted toads live in the southwestern United States and Mexico. Red-spotted toads are carnivorous and eat insects like ants, bees, and beetles. Males make a high-pitched trill with their vocal cords and vocal sac, which can sound like a cricket. Red-spotted toads have large glands called parotoids behind their eyes that secrete toxins. Red-spotted toads are active mainly at night.

Texas toads live in the western two thirds of Texas, as well as parts of Oklahoma and New Mexico. Texas toads live in soft soil and can be found in burrows, under logs, or in cracks in the mud. They grow to about 3.5 inches long. Texas toads can bury themselves in mud or cooler soils to go dormant during hot weather. Texas toads have poor eyesight and can only see bright lights and figures. Texas toads secrete a toxin that can cause respiratory failure in predators. The Texas toad is the state amphibian of Texas.

Fowler's toads are typically 3.5 inches long. They have short legs and dry, warty skin. Fowler's toads are usually brown or gray in color but can also be olive green or brick red. Male Fowler's toads have a distinctive call that sounds like a prolonged shrill or a sheep-like bleat. Fowler's toads live in a variety of habitats across the eastern United States and northern Lake Erie. Fowler's toads are nocturnal and spend most of their time underground, especially during hot or cold weather. They are most active on humid summer evenings.

Amargosa toads can grow to be 4 to 5 inches long. Amargosa toads have smooth skin with warts, a light stripe down their back, and darker stripes or spots on either side. Amargosa toads are rare and only live in the Oasis Valley of Nevada. Their habitat is limited to a 10-mile stretch of the Amargosa River and its surrounding springs and wetlands. Amargosa toads secrete a toxin from their skin that makes them taste bad to other wildlife, dogs, and cats.

common toads in Arizona and Nevada. Arizona toads are often gray or beige with reddish or brown warts. During extreme heat or cold weather, they take refuge in rodent burrows. Arizona toads are inactive in cold weather and are mainly nocturnal. Arizona toads dig under soil, tree roots, and large stones. They also shed their skin and sometimes swallow it. Arizona toads have a parotoid gland that produces a foul-tasting toxin.

with white and tan speckles. Black toads live in the Deep Springs Valley of California. They are mainly aquatic and never stray far from water. They are also known as the Inyo toad or Deep Springs toad. Black toads are active during warmer months and over winter they go underground. They walk rather than hop. Black toads can see in color like humans. They can communicate audibly with each other, but male toads do not have vocal sacs.

Houston toads are 2 to 3.5 inches long. Houston toads are found in a narrow area between Houston, Austin, and Dallas. Houston toads live in loose, deep sands that are at least 40 inches deep. They burrow into the sand to protect themselves from the cold and heat. Houston toads are nocturnal and eat insects and small invertebrates. Males call with a high-pitched trill that sounds like tinkling bells. They are brown, gray, purplish gray, sometimes with green patches. The Houston toad was one of the first amphibians federally listed as an endangered species.

Southern toads can grow to be over 4 inches long. The southern toad is native to the southeastern United States, from eastern Louisiana and southeastern Virginia south to Florida. Southern toads are often brown, but can also be gray, black, or reddish brown. They eat insects and small invertebrates. In the spring, they emerge from hibernation and fill the air with long, trilling calls. When threatened, they make themselves look large and tip their heads downward to expose their parotoid glands. These glands produce bufotoxin, which can be toxic or foul-tasting to predators. Their eggs are also coated in toxin.

blunt snouts and warty skin. Arroyo toads are known for their unique adaptation to living in sandy streambeds, primarily being nocturnal, and unfortunately, being classified as an endangered species due to habitat loss. They are mostly found in California and parts of Mexico, where they burrow deep into the sand during the day to survive harsh conditions, and emerge at night to hunt for insects, mainly ants.

many parts of the USA, including the northern, the Southwest, and parts of southern Canada. Most Leopard frogs have dark spots on their backs and legs. They make a croak call that is a long snoring sound followed by a series of croaks, grunts, or chuckles. They can grow to be 4.5 inches long. Tadpoles have eyes on top of their heads, unlike other frog species. Leopard frogs can jump up to 6 feet. Leopard frogs hibernate in the winter at the bottom of ponds or streams, buried in sediment or under rocks or logs.

Brown leopard frogs, also known as southern leopard frogs, live in many parts of the USA, including northern areas. They are widely spread throughout America. There are different names for Leopard frogs, but whether they are brown or green, they are all part of the leopard frog family, just with different colors. All Leopard frogs are semi-aquatic, living in both water and on land. Like many frogs the Leopard Frog lives near ponds, swamps, slow-moving streams and marshes. It can also be found in well covered grasslands. Leopard frogs will eat just about anything that fits in their mouths.

Gopher frogs use burrows for shelter, that's how they got their name. Gopher frogs are found in the southeastern USA. Gopher frogs come in many shades of green, and they have speckles that help them hide in vegetation. Gopher frog tadpoles can be yellow-green, olive-green, or gray with black spots. Gopher frogs eat a variety of insects. Male gopher frogs make calls that sound like snoring. When threatened, gopher frogs shield their eyes with their hands. Gopher frogs are covered in warts that secrete a milky substance. They can grow to be over four inches long.

Little grass frogs are one of the smallest frogs in North America, measuring 7/16 to 5/8 of an inch long. Their color can be gray, tan, brown, reddish, or brick red, with a dark line on their side. Little grass frogs live in wet, grassy areas near shallow bodies of water. Little grass frogs are found in the Southeastern US, from Virginia to the southern tip of Florida. Little grass frogs can jump up to 20 times their body length. This helps them to escape predators. Their high pitched, insect-like, tinkling call can be heard throughout the year.

Pond frogs, such as the common frog, green frog, and mink frog, can range in size from 2.8 to 4 inches long. There are several different types of pond frogs. There are over 7,000 species of frogs worldwide, and scientists are still discovering new species. Pond frogs live in ponds, marshes, swamps, and other bodies of water. They may also be found in creeks, streams, and slow-moving pools. Most frogs are ectothermic, meaning they can't generate their own body heat.

Columbia spotted frogs can grow to be 3.5 inches long. Columbia spotted frogs live in western North America, from Alaska to parts of Utah, Nevada, and Wyoming. Spotted frogs can be found in areas up to 9850 feet in elevation. They are tan, light to dark brown, gray, or olive-green. Their underside can be white or yellow. They have irregularly shaped black spots on their back and legs. They prefer relatively still freshwater areas, such as ponds, lakes, or slow-moving streams. The tadpoles are born black and have eyes on top of their head. A Columbia spotted frog can jump up to 20 times its body length.

Northern green frogs can grow to be 4.5 inches long. They are the second largest frog in Minnesota and Wisconsin. Northern green frogs live in freshwater habitats in the eastern United States and Canada. They can make up to six different calls, including a yelp when startled, and a call that sounds like a loose banjo string. They are active during the day and at night. They have a large tympanum, or eardrum, behind their eye that vibrates when sound waves hit it.

American bullfrogs are native to the eastern and central USA. Bullfrogs prefer warm, slow, or stagnant waters with lots of vegetation. American bullfrogs are the largest frog in North America, growing up to 8 inches long and weighing up to 1 pound. They are carnivorous and eat a wide variety of animals, including crayfish, fish, snails, birds, and other frogs. Only male bullfrogs croak, making a sound like jug-o-rum. They croak to attract mates and establish territory. Bullfrogs can jump distances 10 times their body length, up to 6 feet.

Rain frogs are known for their defensive squeaking sound and their ability to puff themselves up to appear bigger and more intimidating. Rain frogs can puff up like a balloon to appear more intimidating. Rain frogs can grow to 3 inches long. Rain frogs are native to southern Africa, but some have been released in the USA. Rain frogs have flat, spade-shaped feet that help them dig. Rain frogs lay eggs in shallow underground nests, and the eggs hatch into froglets instead of tadpoles.

Pig frogs get their name from the grunting sound they make, that sounds like a pig grunting. Pig frogs are typically 3 to 6 inches long, with a maximum length of 6.5 inches. Pig frogs live in the southeastern coastal plains of the USA, Pig frogs live in permanent bodies of water, such as ponds, lakes, and marshes. Pig frogs eat crayfish, dragonflies, beetles, and other aquatic invertebrates. Pig frogs move by hopping, leaping, and swimming. Pig frogs burrow into mud at the bottom of ponds or wetlands to hibernate during the winter. Pig frogs have webbing to the tips of their hind feet, to help them swim.

Pickerel frogs are medium-sized frogs that are usually 2 to 4 inches long. Pickerel frogs have two rows of large, dark spots on their back. Pickerel frogs live in the eastern and midwestern USA. Pickerel frogs are the only poisonous frog's native to the USA. Their skin secretions can irritate humans and are fatal to many small animals. Many snakes and mammals avoid pickerel frogs because of their toxic skin secretions. Pickerel frogs make a low nasal snore, like a mooing of a cow. Pickerel frog tadpoles take around three months to turn into frogs.

Southern cricket frogs get their name from the cricket-like call they make. Their call sounds like marbles clicking together. Southern cricket frogs grow to 1.25 inches long. Southern cricket frogs live in the southeastern United States, from Virginia to Florida and east to Louisiana. The frog is beneficial to humans because it consumes pest insects. They are insectivores, eating mainly flies, spiders, beetles, and other small insects. Southern cricket frogs are the smallest frogs in Tennessee. Southern cricket frogs are among the best jumpers in the amphibian world, able to jump over 60 times their body length.

Northern cricket frogs are very small, usually less than 1.5 inches long. They are one of the smallest frogs in North America. Northern cricket frogs live in a wide range of habitats, including ponds, lakes, streams, forests, and grasslands. They are most common in the southeastern United States. Their call sounds like a series of clicks, like two pebbles being tapped together. They are very agile leapers and can jump more than 5 feet for their size. Northern cricket frogs can increase the concentration of glucose in their body fluids to lower their freezing points. This makes them resistant to freezing in colder temperatures.

Blanchard's cricket frogs are small frogs that are usually less than 1.5 inches long. They are the most aquatic tree frog in North America. Blanchard's cricket frogs live in the central and southeastern United States. They are also found in northeastern Mexico. The male Blanchard's cricket frog has a distinctive rasping noise that sounds like two pebbles being rapidly clicked together. They can leap up to 6 feet to escape predators. They can be active in the winter if the weather is not too severe. Their skin is thin and can easily absorb pollutants and other toxins.

often found in the Cascade and Olympic Mountains of Washington, Oregon, and California. They have small bumps on their backs and sides, and their eyes are positioned to the sides. The colors on their backs can change to attract other frogs. They are diurnal, meaning they are active during the day. They are also known to bask on the sun on water-covered rocks. Cascades frogs hibernate during the winter by burrowing into the muddy bottoms of lakes and ponds. Their calls can be low-pitched, grating, and chuckling, or a series of rapid clucks.

or olive front skin with darker colors on their back. American water frogs have streamlined bodies and webbed feet that help them swim. American water frogs are known for their vocalizations, which include croaks, trills, and peeps. They use these sounds to communicate with other frogs. Frogs have excellent night vision and are sensitive to movement. Male frogs have vocal sacs, which are pouches of skin that fill with air.

green tree frogs live throughout the United States in habitats with lots of vegetation and a water source. They are usually green, greenish gray, or yellow green on their backs. Their color can change based on temperature and lighting. They are more active at night. They love to climb trees. They are known for their loud calls that sound like a cowbell from a distance. They call loudest during damp weather, which is why they are good indicators that it's going to rain. They can change their skin color to match their surroundings.

Barking tree frogs can grow to be 2.75 inches long. They are one of the larger treefrogs in North America. They use their suction cup toe pads to climb on all types of surfaces. Barking tree frogs have granular skin on their backs. They can change color from brown to gray, yellow, or various shades of green. They often have dark spots on their backs. A group of barking tree frogs can sound like a pack of barking dogs. When threatened, they inflate with air to appear larger. They have the largest tadpoles of many tree frogs. The Barking Treefrog is sometimes referred to as the rain frog, because its barking call is often heard during rainstorms.

The Pacific treefrog is usually less than 2 inches long. They are native to the Pacific and western regions of North America. They live in a variety of habitats. Their color varies from pale gray to tan, bronze or bright green. They usually have dark patches or stripes on their back and their eyes. They can quickly change their skin color from light to dark to blend in with their surroundings. This helps protect them from predators. The Pacific treefrog is the state frog of Washington State. They make a variety of different calls. They are also known as chorus frogs because of its many sounds it can make.

Squirrel tree frogs are usually 1.5 inches long. They make a raspy sound, that sounds like a gray squirrel's alarm call. They have several color variations, but most commonly they are green. Squirrel tree frogs live in a variety of habitats, including swamps, marshes, and urban areas. They prefer moist areas with shade and lots of insects. They have large, sticky toepads that help them to cling to trees and other surfaces. They are sometimes called rain frogs, because they call loudly after summer showers.

Mexican tree frogs can grow to be 4 inches long. The are one of the largest tree frogs in the United States. Mexican tree frogs are found in Mexico, United States and Costa Rica. They can be green, brown, or light brown with darker patches. Mexican tree frogs are nocturnal and most active after it rains. The male frog makes a wonk wonk, wonk, sound when he sings. They make a high-pitched sound when they sense danger. They can make a cocoon around themselves that stops water from leaving their bodies. They shed the skin cells on the outside of their bodies.

Pine Barrens tree frogs are typically less than 2 inches long. They are named after the New Jersey Pine Barrens. They can be found in the New Jersey Pine Barrens, parts of North Carolina, Alabama, and the western Florida panhandle. They are nocturnal, meaning they come out at night, and they are very seldom seen. Their call sounds like a nasal honk or quonk. They are typically green in color with orange spots on the surfaces of their legs, armpits, and groin.

Cuban tree frogs can grow to be over 6 inches long, making them the largest treefrog in North America. Cuban tree frogs are commonly found in Florida, the Caribbean, Hawaii, and the Bahamas. They can be beige, white, brown, green, or dark yellow. They have large eyes, and toepads that expand to help them climb. They are excellent climbers and can be found high in trees. They are mainly nocturnal and sleep during the day. They secrete a toxic mucus from their skin that can irritate the eyes.

Pine woods tree frogs are usually 1.5 inches long. Pine woods tree frogs live in the southeastern United States, in pine forests, swamps, marshes, and other wetlands. They inflate their throats to make a distinctive, fast croaking sound. They are sometimes called Morse code frogs because of their distinct call. They can have tan, brown, green, or gray skin, and dark markings on their back. They also have a bandit mask band across their eyes. They are opportunistic feeders that eat ants, beetles, crickets, moths, and flies.

California tree frogs are typically 2 inches long from snout to vent. They have rough skin that is often gray or brown with dark blotches. They have an air bladder they fill with air to call with. Their call is a loud quick low-pitched duck-like quacking call. California tree frogs live in California, and Mexico. They can be found in a variety of habitats. California tree frogs have enlarged toe tips for climbing and natural camouflage colors to avoid predators. California tree frogs are nocturnal and are rarely seen in the water unless they are avoiding predators. When disturbed, they jump into water to hide and then return to the shore very quickly.

Canyon tree frogs are usually 2.5 inches long. Canyon tree frogs live in the rocky canyons of the southwestern United States and northern Mexico. They are often found near streams and pools of water. Their color varies from tan to grayish to olive gray. They are well camouflaged, with skin that blends in with rocks. They have bright yellow colors on their sides and thighs that's visible when they jump. They have skin secretions that harden on their body to prevent water loss. These secretions can irritate the eyes and nose of humans. Their call is a loud rapid, stuttering "ah-ah-ah-ah-ah" lasting usually about 2 seconds.

Gray tree frogs are typically 2 inches long. Gray tree frogs live across the eastern United States and parts of southeastern Canada. Gray tree frogs can change their skin color to blend in with their surroundings. The gray tree frog's call is a squeaky chirp or weep that sounds like a bird. They have large, sticky pads on their toes that help them climb. Gray tree frogs hibernate in the winter by freezing themselves. They produce glycerol to protect their body cells and to slow down their metabolism. Adults produce a toxin on their skin that irritates predators. In humans, it can irritate the eyes, lips, inside of the noes, and open cuts or scrapes.

Wright's mountain tree frogs can grow to 2.25 inches. Wright's mountain tree frogs live in the United States and Mexico. Its natural habitats are temperate forests, grasslands, rivers, and freshwater marshes. They are green or coppery brown in color with dark eyestripes, and dark spots on the head and upper back. They are skilled climbers and jumpers because of their long toes and strong legs. They are nocturnal and have large eyes, which helps them to see and navigate in the forest canopy at night.

Strecker's chorus frogs can grow to be about 1.5 inches long. Strecker's chorus frogs live in the south-central United States. They can be Gray, brown, olive, or green with dark spots and dark marks on the cheeks. The Strecker's chorus frog's call is a series of high-pitched, bell-like whistles that are repeated quickly. The call is like the sound of a squeaky wheel, that can be heard up to half a mile away. They are most active at night and spend the day hiding under the soil. They use their front feet to burrow into the ground, which is unusual for frogs. They are difficult to observe because they rarely venture above ground.

Spotted chorus frogs are usually less than 1.25 inches long. Spotted chorus frogs live in the prairies, grasslands, and pastures of central America. They are usually olive green or gray with lighter green mottling on their backs, and white on their undersides. The call of a spotted chorus frog sounds like running a fingernail over the teeth of a comb. It's a series of quick clicks that increases in pitch slightly at the end. Spotted chorus frogs call at night. Chorus frogs can survive being frozen and are among the first frogs to emerge in the spring.

Upland chorus frogs can grow to be 1.5 inches long. Upland chorus frogs live in moist, vegetated areas in the southeastern United States. Upland chorus frogs are usually tan to light brown with darker stripes running down their back and dark lines by their eyes. The call of an upland chorus frog is a series of short, high-pitched trills that is described like a crrreek or prrreep noise. They have small, adhesive pads at the tips of each toe that they use for climbing. Upland chorus frogs are secretive, and are rarely seen or heard except immediately after rains.

Western chorus frogs are typically 1.5 inches long. The Western Chorus Frog is found in the northeastern and central United States and parts of southeastern Canada. They are usually tan or brown with dark eye bands and skin blotches. They are one of the first frogs to start calling in the spring. Their call is a rising cree-ee-ee-eek sound that lasts about 2 seconds and can be heard from half a mile away. They are secretive and rarely seen. They retreat deep into mud to escape the heat of summer.

Ornate chorus frogs are typically 1.5 inches long. Ornate chorus frogs live in the southeastern United States, in pine forests, wetlands, and other habitats. Their call is a rapid, high-pitched, metallic peep, that sounds like a chirping bird or a loose fan belt in a car. Their color is gray, green, reddish-brown, or bright green with dark blotches and a lighter underbody color. They can also have orange on their belly. They are nocturnal and most often seen on rainy nights. They are one of the few frogs that are more active in cooler temperatures or during the winter months.

Wood frogs live in the northeastern United States, including the Upper Midwest, and in the forests of Alaska. Wood frogs are usually three inches long. Wood frogs can survive in freezing temperatures. Wood frogs can freeze and thaw without dying because their bodies use glucose and urea for protection. Wood frogs survive the winter by partially freezing. During this time, their hearts stop beating and they stop breathing. As it warms up, they thaw out and become active again. Wood frogs have glands that secrete a mild toxin onto their skin, but they are not a threat to humans.

Spotted frogs got their name because they have darker spots on their skin. The color of spotted frogs can change with age. They have a bumpy skin texture and are tan to dark olive in color with dark spots that often have light centers. Spotted frogs, including the Columbia spotted frog and the Oregon spotted frog, live in the western USA, from Alaska to California. They grow from 2 to 4 inches long. Female spotted frogs are usually larger than males. They can migrate long distances to find new water sources when their water sources dry up. They have long, sticky tongues that they use to catch and eat insects.

Mink frogs grow to be about 3 inches long. Mink frogs live in the northern USA and Canada. Mink frogs are primarily aquatic and live in cool, slow-moving bodies of water. They are rarely found away from water and only leave at night during rain. They make a rapid cut, cut, cut sound resembling a hammer striking wood. When mink frogs call in chorus it sounds like Horses hooves on a cobblestone road. When handled, they emit a strong rotten onion smelling odor. Tadpoles take about a year before turning into froglets. Mink frogs hibernate in the mud at the bottom of the lake to avoid freezing.

Red-legged frogs can grow up to 5.5 inches long. Red-legged frogs live in California, British Columbia and Mexico. The California red-legged is the largest native frog in the western USA. They live in or near still bodies of water, like ponds, lakes, and marshes. Red-legged frogs are nocturnal, they come out at night and eat insects, small mice, and fish. Most frogs cannot make sounds underwater, but the male red-legged frog can call from underwater or beneath ice. Red-legged frog tadpoles are herbivores that eat plants.

Spring peeper frogs live in the eastern USA and north into southern Canada. Spring peepers are small frogs that are usually 1.5 inches long. Spring peepers have vocal sacs that inflate like balloons to create their high-pitched peeping sounds. Spring peepers can be heard from a mile away. Spring peepers are good climbers due to their large toe pads. Thet Prefer to live in waters without fish. Spring peepers are nocturnal and well-camouflaged. They are more likely to be heard than seen.

Fun Facts About Frogs

1. Frogs and toads are the same thing. There is no distinction between frogs and toads. They are all part of the same family.

2. Frogs have survived on the planet for over 360 million years, surviving several mass extinction events along the way.

3. Frogs have webbed feet that help them swim. The thin layer of skin between their toes helps them push water backward.

4. Frog eggs hatch into tadpoles, which eventually turn into frogs.

5. Frogs have big eyes that give them an almost 180-degree field of vision. They have excellent night vision.

6. Frogs prefer to live in wet environments to keep their skin wet and hydrated. Frogs don't drink water they absorb it through their skin.

7. Some male frogs have vocal sacs, which are pouches of skin that fill with air, so they can make their call.

8. Some frogs can jump more than 20 times their body length.

9. Some frogs and toads, secrete a poison through their skin.

10. Scientists can determine a frog's age by counting the rings that form on its bones during hibernation.

Author Page

Billy Grinslott & Kinsey Marie Books

Copyright, All Rights Reserved

ISBN – 9781965098608

Thanks